# Summary and Analysis

# of

# *The Dichotomy of*

# *Leadership*

*Balancing the Challenges of*

*Extreme Ownership to Lead and*

*Win*

Book Nerd

Copyright © 2018 Book Nerd

All rights reserved.

ISBN: 9781791581855
ISBN-13:

## Our Free Gift to You

We would like to thank you for being a fan and for reading this series with two free books on affirmations and procrastination. Download your free ebooks now:

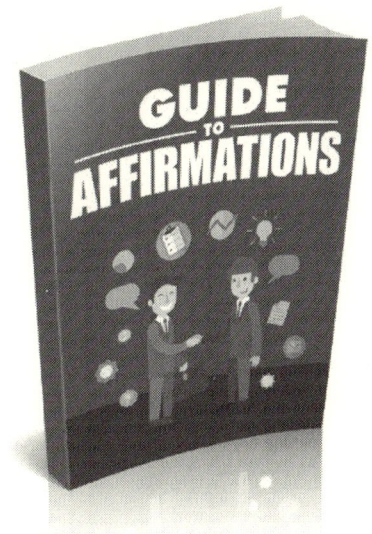

https://www.subscribepage.com/2freemindsetebooks

Sincerely,

    The Book Nerd Team

# TABLE OF CONTENTS

|    | Overview of The Dichotomy of Leadership | Pg #1-3 |
|----|------------------------------------------|---------|
| 1  | Chapter One of The Dichotomy of Leadership | Pg #4-6 |
| 2  | Chapter Two of The Dichotomy of Leadership | Pg #8-11 |
| 3  | Chapter Three of The Dichotomy of Leadership | Pg #12-15 |
| 4  | Chapter Four of The Dichotomy of Leadership | Pg #16-18 |
| 5  | Chapter Five of The Dichotomy of Leadership | Pg #19-21 |
| 6  | Chapter Six of The Dichotomy of Leadership | Pg #23-26 |
| 7  | Chapter Seven of The Dichotomy of Leadership | Pg #27-29 |
| 8  | Chapter Eight of The Dichotomy of Leadership | Pg #30-32 |
| 9  | Chapter Nine of The Dichotomy of Leadership | Pg #33-35 |
| 10 | Chapter Ten of The Dichotomy of Leadership | Pg #36-38 |

| | | |
|---|---|---|
| 11 | Chapter Eleven of The Dichotomy of Leadership | Pg #39-41 |
| 12 | Chapter Twelve of The Dichotomy of Leadership | Pg #42-44 |
| | Background Information on The Dichotomy of Leadership | Pg #45 |
| | About Jocko Willink and Leif Babin | Pg #46-47 |
| | Trivia Questions on The Dichotomy of Leadership | Pg #48-50 |
| | Discussion Questions on The Dichotomy of Leadership | Pg #51-53 |

Note to readers:
This is an unofficial summary & analysis of Willink's and Babin's *The Dichotomy of Leadership*. This summary is designed to enrich your reading experience. Buy the original book here:
https://www.amazon.com/Dichotomy-Leadership-Balancing-Challenges-Ownership-ebook/dp/B079Y51FC3/

Disclaimer: All Rights Reserved. No part of this publication may be reproduced or retransmitted, electronic or mechanical, without the written permission of the publisher; with the exception of brief quotes used in connection in reviews written for inclusion in a magazine or newspaper.

This eBook is licensed for your personal enjoyment only. This eBook may not be re-sold or given away to other people. If you would like to share this book with another person, please purchase an additional copy for each recipient. If you're reading this book and did not purchase it, or it was not purchased for your use only, then please purchase your own copy. Product names, logos, brands, and other trademarks featured or referred to within this publication are the property of their respective trademark holders. These trademark holders are not affiliated with us and they do not sponsor or endorse our publications. This book is unofficial and unauthorized. It is not authorized, approved, licensed, or endorsed by the aforementioned interests or any of their licensees. The information in this book has been provided for educational and entertainment purposes only.

The information contained in this book has been compiled from sources deemed reliable and it is accurate to the best of the Author's knowledge;

# Summary and Analysis of The Dichotomy of Leadership

however, the Author cannot guarantee its accuracy and validity and cannot be held liable for any errors or omissions. Upon using the information contained in this book, you agree to hold harmless the author from and against any damages, costs, and expenses, including any legal fees, potentially resulting from the application of any of the information provided by this guide. The disclaimer applies to any damages or injury caused by the use and application, whether directly or indirectly, of any advice or information presented, whether for breach of contract, tort, neglect, personal injury, criminal intent, or under any other cause of action. You agree to accept all risks of using the information presented inside this book.

The fact that an individual or organization is referred to in this document as a citation or source of information does not imply that the author or publisher endorses the information that the individual or organization provided. This is an unofficial summary & analytical review and has not been approved by the original author of the book.

# OVERVIEW OF THE DICHOTOMY OF LEADERSHIP

"The Dichotomy of Leadership" by Jocko Willink and Leif Babin, is a well-received sequel to "Extreme Ownership: How U.S. Navy SEALs Lead and Win," by the same authors. Both books hold the title of New York Times bestseller, and take a long look at how military experience instills refined leadership qualities in the authors.

This manual for team leadership is divided into three central segments. Each part is then split between four chapters, and each chapter itself is then split in three sections. In each chapter the reader receives: a vivid war story which reflects the discussed principle in action, a brief synthesis of the principle at large, and an example of the principle being applied in everyday business scenarios.

Part one is called *Balancing People*. The first four

chapters analyze a leader's relationship with his subordinates. Part two, titled *Balancing the Mission*, addresses situational awareness and adaptability; leaders must be vigilant of many human elements when running a business. Part two reviews and examines these human conditions. The third and final part of the book is titled *Balancing Yourself*. Slightly self-explanatory, the book concludes with tips for ensuring that the leaders themselves are at their best.

Both of these authors served as Navy SEALs together during the Iraqi conflict, and they do a good job imparting desperate, nerve wracking scenes of Fallujah and Ramadi. After their time in the service, they became leadership consultants, traveling far and wide to help businesses that need leadership training.

Therein lays the narrative counterbalance. After

Summary and Analysis of The Dichotomy of Leadership demonstrating how they came to appreciate a certain aspect of leadership in a war zone, they demonstrate how it can be applied through a retelling of their own business experience. This narrative format of the book, although predictable and repetitive, delivers the message.

# CHAPTER ONE OF THE DICHOTOMY OF LEADERSHIP

Chapter one is titled "The Ultimate Dichotomy" and is written by Jocko Willink. Dichotomy, as the title may suggest, is a theme that will persevere through the entire book. In fact, it could be interpreted as the book's most important, central statement: there is always dichotomy in leadership tactics. This translates, essentially, into too much of a good thing makes it bad. Here the author is reminding the reader that leadership is a constant struggle of checks and balances, of evaluating risk and profit, of managing people, and of making hard decisions.

Here, a story about wounded soldiers is mirrored with that of a failing mining operation. The person operating the mine had too many employees. He had been forced to close another one of his operations due to inefficiency, and he had tried to give about a

Summary and Analysis of The Dichotomy of Leadership

quarter of those employees – whom he would otherwise be letting go – positions at another site. He did this because he cared for their well-being, and didn't want them to face unemployment. Unfortunately, because of this, the mine is losing money, and he is forced to lay off a large number of the transferred employees. This dichotomy, finding the balance between how much to care for employees, is mimicked by an anecdote about the military.

The hardest part about this dichotomy was caring too much. Just as the mining supervisor cared too much about his employees to fire them, the authors care too much about their men to get them killed. Yet that possibility is an inevitability, just like the loss of employment. In America, one can lose one's job in a heartbeat, for reasons like picking their nose to company bankruptcy, and anything in between. As a soldier, one is forced to accept the risk of death every day, and must carry on none the less.

Yet if people need to be fired for the sake of greater company well-being, then that's what needs to be done - just as a soldier must place himself in harm's way to accomplish an important task.

# Summary and Analysis of The Dichotomy of Leadership

# CHAPTER TWO OF THE DICHOTOMY OF LEADERSHIP

"Own It All, but Empower Others" speaks largely with its title. In the second chapter, also written and narrated by Jocko, micromanagement is discussed. The message at the end is clear: find the middle ground. Don't over manage people, but don't let yourself fall out of the loop. Delegation is a powerful tool, even an essential one, the authors argue. In the city of Fallujah, Jocko saw that he was too controlling over the micro aspects of the operation. In turn, this created a lack of personal initiative among his soldiers and a decline in attention to detail. He was able to address this issue by properly delegating, and got great results during an extraction mission.

In this chapter, micromanagement is identified as

Summary and Analysis of The Dichotomy of Leadership

a critical flaw in many leaders. To combat this, Jocko outlines simple directives; a chain of command is essential for leadership to function, and if guidance is required, it is up to the leader to see it done. The central concept is that responsibility for everything rests with the leader, but taking direct command of everything is detrimental. An image that stands out from this chapter is a description of "the easy button." Willink argues that by having an answer to every question, other people in semi-leadership positions have an easy way out. Some might not think for themselves if they don't have to, especially at work. Creating a leadership structure that includes critical thought and responsibility is just as important as having a capable leader at the very top.

For example, imagine the lead singer and figure head of a major, global band. This person originally got the band together, wrote most of the songs, and got the band its first gigs. Now, the band is larger than its members could have ever imagined. The band is constantly looking for new material, a place to sleep, food to eat, transportation, and lugging around the necessary equipment. At first, the lead singer loves doing everything. The band revels in the starlight they have bought themselves through hard work, but this is unsustainable.

Soon the singer is forgetting things like cables in the hotel rooms. The reservations don't get booked correctly, and they are all forced to sleep in the van, yet again. Morale is low. There hasn't been a new song in months. People are hungry. How long was that drive to the next venue?

The singer realizes that it is all far too much to take on just by themselves. The group hires a manager to manage food, transportation, venues, and lodging. They encourage the other band mates

Summary and Analysis of The Dichotomy of Leadership

to take song writing into their own hands. They still hold the position of front men, they are still the leaders of the group, but now the group functions more efficiently. Now people are happy, motivated, and the band flourishes.

# CHAPTER THREE OF THE DICHOTOMY OF LEADERSHIP

Chapter Three opens with a harrowing account of fire. The team is pinned down from devastating machine gun fire and delivered from a friendly tank mistakenly. Radioing the tank's occupants would have been a simple thing, if the radio did not have to be reprogrammed to reach them. Because of this, the team suffered under the friendly fire far longer than they should have. Later, the unit is reprimanded for wearing personalized patches on their uniforms. Eventually, a compromise is reached regarding the patches, for the sake of the men's morale.

The chapter is titled "Resolute, but Not Overbearing," written by author Leif Babin. Here the message is to set high standards, but not to be inflexible. It was a serious issue that the team could

Summary and Analysis of The Dichotomy of Leadership

not reprogram the radios, one that could have been solved by more leadership supervision. However this is balanced by the need to loosen regulation on uniform patches. In the segment about business application, Babin writes that leaders only have so much authority to spend. Where to spend it was something to be carefully considered. At the moment of writing this chapter, Babin was speaking with a company's executive vice president who came down too hard one cell phones.

This section goes discussed the band example from the previous chapter. So now the band has a manager, the members are now missing some of that control the band once had over every piece of the band's mechanics. The lead singer begins to make heavy edits on the others songs, take charge of media appearances, and speaks generally for the whole group. This irritates the band members, and resentment slowly builds until the band becomes unstable.

The others recognize that the lead singer is the best songwriter among them. They don't mind the edits so much, in fact, sometimes they actually enjoy them. This was what the singer did best, after all. The only person who gripped about them was the drummer, who had a sort of knack for songwriting, and wanted it acknowledged. The band does, however, want to be involved in media appearances. They want to speak for themselves in interviews. The singer realizes that his band is right. He is not the sole member of this team; he is only the leader. He continues to edit the songs, but with the drummer's input, and everyone goes on TV together again. The band evens out. The band stands strong behind their goals and aspirations, and the lead singer has high standards for his band, but still listens to their

Summary and Analysis of The Dichotomy of Leadership

feedback. This shows that he's not overbearing but he is firm in his goals and commitment toward making great music.

# CHAPTER FOUR OF THE DICHOTOMY OF LEADERSHIP

The Fourth Chapter, written by Jocko, is called "When to Mentor, When to Fire." Predictably, it deals with under-preforming employees. The authors take a strong stance on mentoring, stating that under-performers shouldn't be fired, they should instead by mentored. Willink's argues that in most cases, reliable support and regular reinforcement will increase the productivity of any employee. Yet occasionally, a leader must let a person go for the good of the company.

    This theme is shown through two lenses: that of a Navy SEAL trainee and a construction site superintendent. Both are good people. They are friendly and have a sustained, positive relationship with their leaders. At the end of the day however,

Summary and Analysis of The Dichotomy of Leadership

neither are fit for their respective jobs, and both have to be fired. While firing is a painful process, it is less painful than the eventual result of continued inadequacies. In the military, Jocko points out, inadequacy can lead to avoidable casualties.

The manager hired in chapter two just isn't quite the best fit for the band. The band is doing great now that they are working so well together, and the manager is struggling to sort out all the new attention. The members even fly to the wrong city one week. Everyone wants to fire the manager after that mistake, especially the drummer.

The lead singer realizes this is a huge mistake, but he is willing to give the manager another chance. He tries to work with the manager to better understand the band, their schedule, and their interests. After three weeks, the manager hasn't improved the way they wanted. He even gets mad at the driver of the tour bus and shouts in frustration, despite the fact that the two have known each other for a long time - the manager introduced the driver to the band in when he was originally hired.

The band decides to fire the manager but panics about finding a replacement. It's important for leaders to know when it's time to fire someone and find a replacement, even if it's not easy. The driver informs the band that he can do the job better, since he has been listening to the old manager blabber on for ten years. The band promotes the driver to manager, hires a new driver, and things go back to being excellent. Better than they were, in fact. This example shows that sometimes it's necessary to give someone with potential a chance and mentor them to take on a new role.

## CHAPTER FIVE OF THE DICHOTOMY OF LEADERSHIP

Chapter Five kicks off part two of the book. "Train Hard, but Train Smart," by Leif Babin, stresses the importance of a rigorous training program. He demonstrates how vital accurate and thorough training can be through the eyes of a soldier. Training, he says, must reflect all possible difficulties. He writes about how it is far better to be humiliated or humbled in a training session than on the battlefield.

This principle applies directly to the business world. In the office setting, Babin recounts the importance of proper training, and helps facilitate a struggling company's executive training program. Here he points out the gravity of both the content and the presenter. Building a training regiment is an organic process full of trial and error, but when properly manifested, it delivers world class results.

Imagine now that the band has written a new, hit song, but it has a series of overly complex chords. The guitarist and bassist have to practice over and over to get it right. They hate to practice this long; they get tired, hungry, irritable, again and again going over the same notes and stumbling in the same places. They go at it for hours and hours until the guitar pick chips from their effort, and they wrap their fingertips in bandages.

But after all that harrowing, brutal practice, they hit the stage, and they are the best they can possibly be. This example shows that hard work is important for accomplishing goals, but working smart is also essential. Otherwise, the band might waste their time working on songs that don't resonate with anyone or waste their time on pointless assignments that don't help the band produce more songs. However, it is better for the musicians to make all

Summary and Analysis of The Dichotomy of Leadership

the embarrassing mistakes during their practice sessions rather than when they're up on stage performing in front of thousands of people. Once the band streamlines their song creation process, they can perform hit songs and their hard efforts will pay off.

# CHAPTER SIX OF THE DICHOTOMY OF LEADERSHIP

Chapter Six, "Aggressive, Not Reckless," by Willink, is all about problem solving. Jocko states that in order to be successful, one must be aggressive, but not reckless. He defines aggression as proactive, not involving anger or temper. To Willink, a successful leader is aggressive by default.

They don't wait to act; they overcome obstacles, seize apparent opportunities, and make forward progress. Instead of waiting for instruction, or being passive, an aggressive leader is always actively trying to solve the problem. The dichotomy here lays in overconfidence. Moving too fast, or being too aggressive, can lead to miscalculation, oversight, and financial ruin.

The author describes a business with an

Summary and Analysis of The Dichotomy of Leadership

extremely aggressive CEO. She is driven, smart, articulate, and ambitious. Nervous about a large expansion, Willink reviews her plans and finds that she has been *too* aggressive. Her budget relied on non- existent funds: the funds that only existed based on her projections. If these projections fail or don't actualize, this would impact the entire budged negatively. By adjusting for risk and coming up with a more realistic projected budged, she was able to expand successfully and aggressively.

Back to the example about the band; the band is now attempting to organize their first international tour. The members are highly ambitious. On a map of the globe they have selected thirty cities they want to visit and know they will have a great reception in. In drafting up this thirty city itinerary, they have overextended their travel budget. They compensate for this by allocating funds from projected royalty sales for the months of the tour.

When presenting this plan to their new manager, they are confronted with some difficulty. The manager explains that they cannot plan on these projected sales. They might be too optimistic about their projected royalties. While they are traveling, their sales spike due to sales in areas that they visit, but sales in other places they tour are not as high. Not to mention, costs may spring up at any point during travel. The numbers they have generated account for a spike in sales everywhere. They cannot make the tour of thirty cities the way they want to, but the manager praises their determination.

A plan is proposed for twenty cities that allows for an emergency budget, and the tour goes remarkably well. This means that the band aggressively pursues their tour goals, but it is not reckless. It's a good idea to prepare for the worst but expect the best. The band didn't give up on their tour goals, and they still persevered, but they had to pivot their plans to ensure that they won't get into financial trouble.

# CHAPTER SEVEN OF THE DICHOTOMY OF LEADERSHIP

Chapter Seven, also written by Willink, is titled "Disciplined, Not Rigid." He writes that discipline is the equivalent of freedom. He goes on to explain how the more drilled and disciplined his unit was, the more creative freedom they had on the battlefield. They were able to adapt situationally, but also could rely on each other's predictability.

Too many regulations, he cautions, can of course be overpowering. Like every other lesson in the book, this chapter comes with its own dichotomy. A balance must be maintained between team members' individual freedom and rigid discipline.

How regulation and freedom relate to the band: the band has been having trouble getting everybody together to practice. The lead singer is terribly frustrated. Since the band started becoming widely

Summary and Analysis of The Dichotomy of Leadership

successful, they have all received much more individual attention from a variety of sources. Band members are now often out with new friends, or partying too hard with their old ones to make it to practice. They insist that the can practice on the tour bus.

The lead singer knows this is an issue. He knows that everyone needs to get together and sit down to play in a stable space at least four times a week. In other words, the band needs to be more disciplined. Although the other band members find this to be too demanding of their time, after a band meeting, a compromise is reached among the team. The lead singer will organize two practice sessions a week, each one extra-long, and the rest of the time would be free. Happy that the leader is no longer demanding too much regulation, the rest of the band obliges to the new schedule and the band's music actually improves. The band leader was wise enough to be disciplined, but he wasn't rigid in carrying out his plan for the band to become more disciplined. He listened to his fellow band members and came up with a plan for discipline that the band members agreed with.

# CHAPTER EIGHT OF THE DICHOTOMY OF LEADERSHIP

Jocko goes on to write Chapter Eight, "Hold People Accountable, but Don't Hold Their Hands," in which he describes his unit's overwhelming success. They were such an effective force, that many soldiers began neglecting equipment on missions in order to move faster. This soon became a serious issue, with some soldiers even omitting their body armor. Through emotional and educational appeal, Jocko was able to convince his men to once again wear the armor.

Leaders must hold team members accountable, he argues, in order for team members to hold themselves accountable. This can be achieved through education and empowerment. He goes on to describe a service provider that struggled with accountability. Upon investigation, he found that the "front line troops," as he called the service technicians, had difficulties with equipment and motivation. After listening to employee feedback, and implementing needed changes that responded to the aggrieved party, things seemed to straighten out.

The band is now a global hit. Everywhere they go people love them. They are millionaires. The only thing going wrong for them is that they haven't written any new songs. The leader has a major case of writers' block and so do the band mates. For a while, the lead singer tries to work with them to produce songs, in order to make sure everyone is spending as much time on songwriting as they need to. The band finds this overbearing and strange.

Responsively, the leader backs off a bit. He also stop reminding the band about new songs

Summary and Analysis of The Dichotomy of Leadership

constantly, and has to trust that they will get it done on their own time. In a band meeting, the lead singer softly explains how important each member is to the band, and how important songs are to the band's future. Understanding why the lead singer had been pressuring them so much, the band mates happily write songs in their own time. The lead singer holds the band accountable for working on new songs, but he doesn't hold their hand. He nudges the band and explains the importance of producing new songs.

# CHAPTER NINE OF THE DICHOTOMY OF LEADERSHIP

Chapter Nine, by Leif Babin, is titled "A Leader and a Follower." In it, Babin goes on to detail a leader's relationship with his team. He recounts a mission to establish a forward operating base, in which he learned a great deal by ceding some command to another. Babin claims that in order to lead effectively, one must also be able to follow. Having learned valuable lessons, he is able to effectively lead his men away from danger later on.

A good leader does not dismiss important insight, nor ignore critical concepts. It is crucial for a leader to learn from, and sometimes lean on his team members. It is just as crucial for those team members to follow their leader loyally. Failure to do so brings resentment. The moral is hit home by a story about a business man who unintentionally

# Summary and Analysis of The Dichotomy of Leadership

intimidated his boss. To fail as a follower is to fail as a leader as well.

This section is about how being a follower applies to the band. The band is hard at work writing songs for the next album. Everyone has taken to their work joyfully ever since the pep talk mentioned in chapter eight. The drummer, especially, is excited about the work. The drummer feels that the band members are good songwriters, and has written a complicated song that they present to the lead singer.

The lead signer is initially put off by the song. It is all a little too much for him to understand. He thanks the drummer but doesn't really give the song the time of day. This creates animosity between the drummer and the lead singer. Finally, after being tired of having his song ignored, the drummer confronts the lead singer and plays the song in its entirety. The lead singer realizes that the song is excellent, and that he was wrong to disregard it. The lead singer goes back over the music with the drummer, and the two of them produce an ever better song that goes on to be the hit of the album.

## CHAPTER TEN OF THE DICHOTOMY OF LEADERSHIP

"Plan, but Don't Overplan" deals with the importance of proper preparation and the dangers of over planning. The Tenth Chapter of the book, written by Babin, depicts an event from his military career. In an effort to be prepared for any situation, he over packed his bag which put too much weight on him both literally and figuratively. This made him a liability to the unit's cohesion. Later, he is able to balance his fear of being unprepared with practicality, and makes a good call in an important moment, saving many lives.

While trying to assist a company that is rapidly expansion, Babin hits on the lesson's dichotomy. You cannot plan for everything. Of course there should be a contingency plan, but there's no need for five of them. By eliminating excess planning from the company's projections, the business was able to thrive through its expansion.

In terms of the band, the album release party is going to be a huge event. A massive space has been reserved, and now it had to be filled with food, drinks, and lights. While planning for the party, the lead singer starts to overthink things. He start to plan for the most unlikely of situations. What if the disco ball falls? We should have an area roped off underneath it. What if there is a power outage? We should have at least two backup generators, in case one isn't enough to power everything. Is there enough food? We should double the orders.

When presenting his fears to the manager, the manager puts the singer at ease. The disco ball was mounted with steel cable. The building had its own generators. There was going to be too much food as it was. The lead singer realized that they only needed to plan practically, and not overthink their

Summary and Analysis of The Dichotomy of Leadership

plans. After this realization, the party becomes fun and well planned. It's not overplanned.

# Book Nerd

# CHAPTER ELEVEN OF THE DICHOTOMY OF LEADERSHIP

Chapter Eleven, called "Humble, Not Passive," is also by Babin. He recounts how the constant combat in Iraq had humbled him and his unit. Each time they attempted to adapt, something new came up which challenge them. One must look beyond one's own personal needs is the central message of this chapter. This message is reflected in a story about a sniper who was assigned by a special task force and given the chance to leave Babin's company. While it would have bettered the man's career to join the special task force, he was too important to the whole of the unit, and so he remained with Babin.

The author writes that the most common reason a SEAL was relieved of duty was due to a lack of humility. He goes on to detail a business in which there was a lack of responsibility and humility in the

Summary and Analysis of The Dichotomy of Leadership

workplace. After careful facilitation, communication between the necessary parties ensued, ending the animosity building up between workplace egos.

The problem of humility has haunted the lead singer ever since the band's success began to take off. The singer sees himself as the one who was mainly responsible for the band's sudden success. The members were emboldened by media appearances and magazine articles. They become slightly self-obsessed because of all the attention they got and regularly clashed with the drummer regarding new songs.

Everyone else was starting to get sick of this behavior too. The team remembers when the lead singer was taking too much control of the band, and that was bad enough. Now the lead singer was making every decision in the band without his superiority in check. He seemed to just think of himself as correct one hundred percent of the time.

The lead singer carried on this way for a bit, until he realize that he had lost his band mates as friends. He has alienated them through his over confidence and pride. The lead singer humbly apologizes for his recent behavior, making sure everyone understands how much he values their friendship. The band makes up. The singer is no longer overly arrogant, and they go on making hit music. The lead singer doesn't act like he's the most important person in the band anymore, but he also doesn't act weak. He remains a strong leader, moving the band forward, but he isn't egotistical anymore.

Summary and Analysis of The Dichotomy of Leadership

# CHAPTER TWELVE OF THE DICHOTOMY OF LEADERSHIP

The final chapter is Chapter Twelve, "Focused, but Detached," by Leif Babin. This final piece examines the dichotomy of focus in leadership positions. The author describes an extraction mission in which he was so caught up with the specifics that he lost track of the greater picture. In order to later plan a successful combat mission, he was forced to detach from the endless details, and look at the larger picture. The final dichotomy layers in that attention to detail. While too much detail will bog you down, distracting you detrimentally, not enough will leave you without a complete overview. In the case of too much or too little, the fault falls entirely on the leader.

The album that the band has been working on has failed to meet the deadline. The lead singer has kept it in the production booth for far too long, going over notes one little bit at a time. The leader wants everything to be perfect, and he wants it to go out into the world flawlessly. So he sits there, night after night, even after the deadline has passed, clicking away on the computer.

The producers are starting to get anxious. It's been too long since the promised release date, and people have begun to cancel their pre-release purchases. The band is nervous because they are all huge spenders, and they are counting on the money from the release.

One day, a few band members go to the singer with their producers. They explain that the signer has been very focused on the details of the music, and that they have forgotten their financial security was on the line. Not just theirs, but everyone else's in the band. Even the music company's security is on

Summary and Analysis of The Dichotomy of Leadership

the line. With such a reality check, the singers quickly wraps up their work. It had probably been read weeks ago, they admit. They agree to keep their mind on the larger picture in the future, and the band is later admitted into the Rock and Roll hall of fame.

# BACKGROUND INFORMATION ON THE DICHOTOMY OF LEADERSHIP

Published September 25th, 2018, by Macmillan publishing, "The Dichotomy of Leadership" instantly shot to the top of the New York Times bestseller list. *Dichotomy* was released approximately three years after the duo's first book, *Extreme Ownership*, which also received national attention.

The work was hailed widely, and quickly, as an emotional piece of true, life insight. Babin and Willink co-authored the book while at their company, Echelon Front. The book reads as an answer to the first book, playing on the previously mentioned lessons and dichotomies. It will likely be a widely circulated piece of leadership literature for years to come in business circles.

Summary and Analysis of The Dichotomy of Leadership

## ABOUT JOCKO WILLINK AND LEIF BABIN

Leif Babin and Jocko Willink both served together in the U.S. Navy SEALs. Both are military men, and can list distinguished careers there before moving into the private sector. Babin, who graduated from the U.S. Naval Academy, served thirteen years in the Navy, nine of which were in the SEALs. During that time he was awarded a silver star, two bronze stars, and a purple heart for his distinguished service. As a platoon commander, Leif planned and facilitated major combat operations during the Battle of Ramadi in 2006.

After leaving active duty, Babin co-founded the company called Echelon Front with Jocko Willink. Willink, who served some twenty years in the Navy, enjoyed a highly decorated military career since he joined as a young man. Their unit, Task Unit Bruiser, was one of the most effective combat forces in the

Battle of Ramadi. Willink played soccer in high school, and he grew up in New England. After the service, he was glad to collaborate with Babin on their company, Echelon Front.

Echelon Front is a leadership training company, hired by other companies to educate their employees on leadership qualities. The company has been hugely successful across the private sector and consists largely of former Navy SEALs.

Leif Babin is married to Jenna Lee, a noted American Journalist, and the couple has two children. Babin's father is U.S. Representative Brain Babin, from Texas. Jocko Willink is an avid practitioner of Brazilian Jujitsu, and hosts a popular podcast on the subject, in addition to his position as co-founder of Echelon Front. Willink's podcast also includes discussions about the military and his own personal philosophies about leadership.

Summary and Analysis of The Dichotomy of Leadership

# TRIVIA QUESTIONS ON THE DICHOTOMY OF LEADERSHIP

1. What are the twelve dichotomies of leadership?

2. How can you tell if an employee should be fired or mentored?

3. How can you help guide people towards accountability?

4. According to *Dichotomy,* what is a leader's most important attribute?

5. How can you tell if you are over planning?

6. What are the seven principles of a successful business relationship with your superior?

7. How do you deal with animosity within the team?

8. If you want to encourage independent initiative among team members, what is the best way to do so?

9. What role does delegation play in the

leadership spectrum?

10. What does "OPORD" stand for?

11. What is the book's motto concerning training?

12. What is the name of the authors unit?

13. What is the custom patch that the unit wears on their uniforms?

14. What are the dangers of being too aggressive in a business setting?

15. According to the book, what role does training play in a business?

16. What was the Battle of Ramadi?

17. What was the required deployment ratio between Iraqi government soldiers, and soldiers from the United States, as described in the book?

18. What happens in a business when a leader applies too much regulation over team members?"

Summary and Analysis of The Dichotomy of Leadership

19. What is the nature of the division between the three parts of the book?

20. How does one find the balance between any of these dichotomies?

# DISCUSSION QUESTIONS ON THE DICHOTOMY OF LEADERSHIP

1. Do you find these principles applicable to your own life experiences? Why or why not?
2. Do you find the authors to be credible narrators? If not, what impact does this have on the text?
3. How do you respond to the mirroring of war stories and business experiences? Does this impact your interpretation of the text?
4. What is the most important thing you gained from this reading? Why do you find it so compelling?
5. Do you agree or disagree with any of the principles as a generality? Why or why not?
6. Do you intend to use any of this information in the future? Why or why not?
7. How do your personal ideas about leadership

Summary and Analysis of The Dichotomy of Leadership

compare to the authors?

8. How does this book affect your interpretation of the military, or the ongoing conflict in Iraq?

9. If you could ask the authors anything, what would it be and why?

10. Would you recommend this book to a friend? Why or why not?

11. Do you feel more adept as a leader after reading this book? Why or why not?

12. What was your favorite story told by either of the authors? Explain your choice.

13. Do you think that the authors practice their own principles accurately in the stories? Why or why not?

14. Do any of the principles oppose each other? Explain you answer.

15. What is the most important quality of leadership to you? Elaborate.

16. Are these principles of leadership easily identifiable in a person?

17. Do you find the morals of each chapter easily discernible? Why or why not?

18. Did you enjoy the book overall? Explain your reasoning.

19. If you could make your own list of leadership qualities, would they overlap with the ones described here?

20. Do you want to be a leader? Why or why not?

## Thank you for reading!

We hope you learned something interesting from this summary.

We care about your reading experience here at Book Nerd and want to provide you with thorough and insightful book guides.

We'd like to give you a virtual high five for reading until the very end. You're a great reader!

Before we part ways, do you mind leaving us a review on Amazon? We would appreciate that greatly, and your support will help us create more book guides in the future.

Thanks again!

Yours Truly,

Book Nerd Team


## Don't forget your gift!

https://www.subscribepage.com/2freemindsetebooks

Book Nerd

# Summary and Analysis of The Dichotomy of Leadership

## ABOUT BOOK NERD

Book Nerd is dedicated to providing readers with thorough and thoughtful summaries.

Made in the USA
Middletown, DE
30 May 2023